self-love 101:
art is healing

Copyright © 2019 by Empriś Durden,
All rights reserved.

No part of this book may be reproduced in any
form or by any electronic or mechanical means,
including information storage and retrieval systems,
without written permission from the author, except
for the use of brief quotations in a book review.

Published by:
Sun Poetry Press

ISBN: 978-0-578-51248-8

For press and business inquiries, contact the author:
E-mail: emprisdurdenpoetry@gmail.com

Website: emprisdurden.com
Instagram: @empris.durden
Twitter: @emprisdurden

dedicated to my mother and father.

to those who came before me:
nayyirah waheed. warsan shire. alex elle. rupi kaur.
yrsa daley-ward. upile chisala. sonia sanchez.
julia cameron.

thank you for making me believe.

dear reader,
i wrote this for you.

empriś durden

self-love 101: art is healing

clean up on aisle my life is in shambles

empriś durden

self-love 101: art is healing

how are you?
they want me in a jail cell or a coffin

empriś durden

self-love 101: art is healing

do we ever really heal?

empriś durden

self-love 101: art is healing

do we ever really heal

empriś durden

self-love 101: art is healing

you know, there's this really cool new show on tv right now,
oh, all those life-changing things?
they can wait

— volen c.k.

empriś durden

self-love 101: art is healing

I said, "I think there's something wrong with me, ma."
She said, "Yeah, maybe."

empriś durden

self-love 101: art is healing

breakdowns are really just breakthroughs

empriś durden

self-love 101: art is healing

rebuilding myself
sketchbook by sketchbook
poem by poem

empriś durden

self-love 101: art is healing

is there an emoji for self-respect

empriś durden

self-love 101: art is healing

shopping list:
something that will make him stay

empriś durden

self-love 101: art is healing

do the echoes of who you always wanted to be keep you up at night too or is it just me

empriś durden

self-love 101: art is healing

the only way out is through

empriś durden

self-love 101: art is healing

healing crystal cereal
crunches
(and sparkles)
as i chew.

empriś durden

self-love 101: art is healing

i'm writing for my life

empriś durden

self-love 101: art is healing

best believe,
i'm writing for my life

empriś durden

self-love 101: art is healing

but if you're happy they can't sell you things

empriś durden

self-love 101: art is healing

the only thing i'm afraid of in this life is lying in my coffin with all this locked up inside of me

empriś durden

self-love 101: art is healing

don't run from the pain,
sit it down and ask it how its day was

make it breakfast

empriś durden

self-love 101: art is healing

hold hands with the pain
lean into it

empriś durden

self-love 101: art is healing

this moment is more precious than you think

empriś durden

self-love 101: art is healing

why are you so afraid of dying?
when the yesterday you dies with each morning

empriś durden

self-love 101: art is healing

but don't cha know?
we are always dying
all of the time

empriś durden

self-love 101: art is healing

i'm sorry, i mistook myself for your type of girl

empriś durden

self-love 101: art is healing

if he wants to go, let him go

empriś durden

self-love 101: art is healing

tell your son be careful i just might put him in a book

empriś durden

self-love 101: art is healing

for a minute there i was so fulfilled that i forgot i was supposed to be looking for a husband

note to self: create more of those moments

empriś durden

self-love 101: art is healing

do not accept scraps of affection;
we are not in slavery times any more

empriś durden

self-love 101: art is healing

"Only remind them once."
— instagram proverb.

via @my_truth_told

empriś durden

self-love 101: art is healing

don't mind me,
just tapping into the power of my ancestors

empriś durden

self-love 101: art is healing

don't mind me,
just a young black artist trying to make a living out here

empriś durden

self-love 101: art is healing

don't mind me,
just a young black writer out here hustling

empriś durden

self-love 101: art is healing

don't mind me,
just a young black dancer out here healing from an injury

empriś durden

self-love 101: art is healing

don't mind me,
just a young black model out here dodging vitriolic online hate

empriś durden

self-love 101: art is healing

just a young black woman out here surviving somehow

empriś durden

self-love 101: art is healing

just a young black youtuber out here posting videos every week please like and subscribe

k thx bai

empriś durden

self-love 101: art is healing

I must admit that I'm arrogant,
there are worse coats to wear.
in a cold winter,
there are worse coats to wear

empriś durden

self-love 101: art is healing

"hey baby, what's your fantasy?"

a committed loving monogamous relationship in which my partner and i both feel respected and uplifted

empriś durden

self-love 101: art is healing

is there an emoji for absolving yourself of guilt through deflecting blame

empriś durden

self-love 101: art is healing

how are you?
self-medicating with art and poetry.

empriś durden

self-love 101: art is healing

your spirit cannot be contained by palaces;
so why do they conscript you to a paper cup?

empriś durden

self-love 101: art is healing

i gave myself permission

empriś durden

self-love 101: art is healing

my enemies aspire to taste of my scraps,
oh, how they clamor to sip of my dishwater.

empriś durden

self-love 101: art is healing

my enemies squirm underfoot

empriś durden

self-love 101: art is healing

my enemies lose sleep over my success.
oh, how they toss and turn

empriś durden

self-love 101: art is healing

my enemies flounder and splinter under questioning

empriś durden

self-love 101: art is healing

you speak to me of writing
as if i had a choice

empriś durden

self-love 101: art is healing

they said, "look inward,"
so i did.

i have not yet recovered from the sight

empriś durden

self-love 101: art is healing

i am slowly replacing my destructive habits with
transformative ones

empriś durden

self-love 101: art is healing

a lot of people look for love in others when we should really look inward and upward

empriś durden

self-love 101: art is healing

i alchemy my pain into poems

empriś durden

self-love 101: art is healing

no, I can't let this pain go to waste.

empriś durden

self-love 101: art is healing

she's a dangerous woman.
she's a defiant woman.
cut her down, i say.

cut her down to size.

empriś durden

self-love 101: art is healing

i feel like i missed a really important lesson in school
you know, the one where they teach you to manipulate
people and whatnot

everyone else is so good at it

empriś durden

self-love 101: art is healing

"they hate me cuz they ain't me."
— dad

empriś durden

self-love 101: art is healing

tropicana lanes
orange and teal waves
of teal and orange

beautiful orbs
glowing spheres of heavy
planets of childhood

galaxies of dad's broken finger dreams

with nostalgia shining all through
full well

empriś durden

self-love 101: art is healing

i'll have the casual pervasive sense of despair
with a side dipping sauce of hope please

empriś durden

self-love 101: art is healing

wi-fi password idea: the entire holy bible

empriś durden

self-love 101: art is healing

note to self: paint a papaya

empriś durden

self-love 101: art is healing

there's no one like me

empriś durden

self-love 101: art is healing

i tried to tell them
there's no one like me

empriś durden

self-love 101: art is healing

don't be fooled
there's no one like me

empriś durden

self-love 101: art is healing

will gladly provide specific examples upon request

empriś durden

self-love 101: art is healing

skip over negativity like video ads, sis

empriś durden

self-love 101: art is healing

they thought i was k.o. but i was just restin' fam

empriś durden

self-love 101: art is healing

you don't need their approval

empriś durden

self-love 101: art is healing

live your life as if everyone will default on their promises

empriś durden

self-love 101: art is healing

relationship status:
married to my art

empriś durden

self-love 101: art is healing

lunch with spirituality be like a fresh spring salad

empriś durden

self-love 101: art is healing

hey (what's up)!

just your friendly ex here checking in to see if you're still on my emotional leash or nah

empriś durden

self-love 101: art is healing

nah

empriś durden

self-love 101: art is healing

oh, okay.

cool.

empriś durden

self-love 101: art is healing

he said,
"do you want to get some sushi?"

i said, "nah.
i have a date tomorrow,

with a brush and canvas."

empriś durden

self-love 101: art is healing

they only want me when i'm up

empriś durden

self-love 101: art is healing

everyone has their medicine
best believe, everyone has their medicine

empriś durden

self-love 101: art is healing

cute first date idea: overthrowing capitalism

empriś durden

self-love 101: art is healing

i'd like to call this class: how to catch a man 101

empriś durden

self-love 101: art is healing

hello, class, welcome to
how to keep a man 101

empriś durden

self-love 101: art is healing

welcome to the first module of your online course:
how to trap a man 101

empriś durden

self-love 101: art is healing

please turn in your final exams.
thank you.

i hope you've learned a lot this semester in
false ultimatums,
empty demands, and
dodging commitment 101

empriś durden

self-love 101: art is healing

i take myself on the best dates
the kind of dates where i leave with manuscripts and mandalas

empriś durden

self-love 101: art is healing

*
dating is like shopping for human souls

empriś durden

self-love 101: art is healing

a man
cannot
save
you.

empriś durden

self-love 101: art is healing

that's funny i don't remember you hitting me up when i was down and out

empriś durden

self-love 101: art is healing

and, you know,
I'd like to think,

I'm a woman worth being fired for

empriś durden

self-love 101: art is healing

He said, "You're selfish."
I said, "I'm healing."

empriś durden

He said, "You don't seem like a happy person."
She said, "I'm not, but I'm working on it."

empriś durden

self-love 101: art is healing

"my bronze adonis"

he was beautiful, with gold thread hair and marble skin. my aluminum titanium platinum diamond man. he gave me cubic zirconium kisses and hugs made of stolen pipe copper. his silver sapphire eyes gleamed whenever i touched him. yes, my adonis was bronze, my man was grand, my man was metal, like the pole he beat me with

empriś durden

self-love 101: art is healing

my adonis was bronze
my man was grand
he was all metal
like the pole he beat me with

empriś durden

self-love 101: art is healing

he's got that hollow sham(wow) smile.
all the girls love it.

empriś durden

self-love 101: art is healing

he's got that hollow sham shamwow smile.
teeth so sharp so shiny so mmm

empriś durden

self-love 101: art is healing

he gave me Swarovski Crystal kisses
he was a cubic zirconia man

empriś durden

self-love 101: art is healing

he had that prismacolor smile
aura so bright so aqua so pink so mm
everytime i hope it hurts so bad

empriś durden

self-love 101: art is healing

the oldest poem in the history of the world:

he lied
he lied
he lied

empriś durden

self-love 101: art is healing

"digitized aurora borealis sound /
when moves he I watch but help I cannot"

when he moves,
I can't help but watch.

he makes a piano flood the room with
digitized aurora borealis sound,

green green jagged blue
flood of peach red soaks their souls,

he walks, can you call it walking?
he floats.
he talks, can you call it talking?
he converts.

when he moves I can't help but watch,
when moves he I watch but help I cannot

empriś durden

self-love 101: art is healing

the quiet defiance in her eyes twinkled in the light
angering some and driving others to
reckless lovestruck passion

empriś durden

self-love 101: art is healing

i went soul shopping but i need a return

empriś durden

self-love 101: art is healing

They say He's a Healer, and,
I stand over her casket

empriś durden

self-love 101: art is healing

They say He's a Healer, and,

empriś durden

self-love 101: art is healing

They say He's a Healer, and,

standing over the casket, I'm asking,
they say He's a Healer, and, I think it's all habit,
they say "how are you?", I say I'm fantastic,
"what else?", there's too many facets to ad-lib,

flower baskets, they kept it classic,
out of my tax bracket, nervous sips from the flask-es,
fidgeting with the gadgets, pulling on my jacket,
cleaned off my glasses, this service is lasting,
it wasn't an assassin, or a crime of passion,
it wasn't a hatchet, or something tragic,
my smile is plastic, there's so many maggots,
we throw her ashes, like it's damascus,
this future is blasted, I need a straitjacket,
i wanna try acid, but let's not be drastic,
now she's dancing in heaven, her hips are now elastic,

They say He's a Healer, you catch it?
They say He's a Healer, the fastest.
They say He's a Healer, and,

empriś durden

self-love 101: art is healing

They say He's a Healer, and,
They say He's a Healer, and,
They say He's a Healer, and,
They say He's a Healer, and,

empriś durden

self-love 101: art is healing

performative grief

empriś durden

self-love 101: art is healing

black raindrops falling upward

empriś durden

self-love 101: art is healing

decorating ourselves with powder and almostmetals
forgetting to eyeline and mascara our character

empriś durden

self-love 101: art is healing

don't try
you'll never find another girl like me

empriś durden

self-love 101: art is healing

i am the next black woman to reach 1 million

empriś durden

self-love 101: art is healing

To those who wished me harm, who threw daggers in my path:
Thank you, you made me better

empriś durden

self-love 101: art is healing

He said, "You're too much."
I said, "I'm just enough."

empriś durden

self-love 101: art is healing

hello, can i schedule a wakeup call?

sure, what time sir?

oh, well time and space are a social construct
so i guess about never

empriś durden

self-love 101: art is healing

hello i want to request a wakeup call

yes, sir, what time?

oh, about 15 years from now, when my wife has left
me, my kids are overgrown failures, and my job adds no
fulfillment or purpose to my short and meaningless life
i suppose, around the middle of my life?

of course, sir. thanks for choosing the westward and onward
suites. good evening.

empriś durden

self-love 101: art is healing

copic grave markers

empriś durden

self-love 101: art is healing

body paint as jewelry

empriś durden

self-love 101: art is healing

I was not made for this world, I say,
You were not made for this world, He said,
We were not made for this world!

We were not made for this world!

I should have believed Him,
The first time.

empriś durden

self-love 101: art is healing

riace warriors

silver eyelashes
copper mouth
ivory teeth

the riace warriors

empriś durden

self-love 101: art is healing

rolling vistas in my visage,
as far as the eye can see

empriś durden

self-love 101: art is healing

(111)*

pastoral interludes for breakfast

*one hundred and eleven

empriś durden

self-love 101: art is healing

if you liked this book,
please leave a 5 star review on amazon

empriś durden

about the author

i am a post-post-modern + self-love poet
living in los angeles, california.

follow me on social media for daily poems:
instagram: @empris.durden
twitter: @emprisdurden

go to emprisdurden.com/free for a free chapbook

Made in the USA
Monee, IL
21 July 2023